W9-BLY-783

American Lives

DISCARD

Mae Jemison

Elizabeth Raum

Heinemann Library
Chicago, Illinois

© 2006 Heinemann Library
a division of Reed Elsevier Inc.
Chicago, Illinois

Customer Service 888-454-2279
Visit our website at www.heinemannlibrary.com

All rights reserved. No part of this publication
may be reproduced or transmitted in any form
or by any means, electronic or mechanical, including
photocopying, recording, taping, or any information
storage and retrieval system, without permission
in writing from the publisher.

Designed by Joanna Hinton-Malivoire and
Q2A Creative

Printed in China by
WKT Company Limited

10 09 08 07 06
10 9 8 7 6 5 4 3 2 1

Library of Congress Cataloging-in-Publication Data
Raum, Elizabeth.
 Mae Jemison / Elizabeth Raum.-- 1st ed.
 p. cm. -- (American lives)
 Includes bibliographical references and index.
 ISBN 1-4034-6942-3 (hc) -- ISBN 1-4034-6949-0
(pb) 1. Jemison, Mae, 1956---Juvenile literature. 2.
African American women astronauts--Biography--
Juvenile literature. 3. Astronauts--United

States--Biography--Juvenile literature.
I.Title. II. Series:
TL789.85.J46R38 2005
629.45'0092--dc22

                    2005006254

Acknowledgments
The author and publishers are grateful to the
following for permission to reproduce
copyright material: Corbis title page, pp. 5, 7, 11
(John Zich), 12 (Dave Butow), 16, 28 (Marc Asnin);
Corbis/Bettmann pp. 15, 19; Getty Images pp. 8, 27
(Robert Mora); Getty Images/AFP p. 23; Getty
Images/Time-Life Pictures p. 22; NASA p. 13;
NASA/Johnson Space Center cover, pp. 4, 17, 18,
20, 21; NASA/Johnson Space Center--Earth Sciences
and Image Analysis p. 26; Scholastic Press pp. 6, 9,
10; Science Photo Library pp. 24, 25, 29

Every effort has been made to contact copyright
holders of any material reproduced in this book.
Any omissions will be rectified in subsequent
printings if notice is given to the publisher.

The photograph on the cover is an official NASA
portrait of Mae C. Jemison, wearing a launch entry suit.

Contents

R0410273528

Some words are shown in bold, **like this.** You can find out what they mean by looking in the glossary.

Stars

September 12, 1992, was no ordinary day for Mae Jemison. She woke up early, showered, and dressed. Then she joined the crew of the space shuttle *Endeavor* for breakfast and a trip into space. Dr. Jemison buckled into her seat on *Endeavor.* After months of training, she was ready for

Mae Jemison was the first African-American woman in space.

liftoff. Moments after launch, the **commander** called Dr. Jemison to come forward and look out the window at Chicago, her hometown. It passed out of sight in less than five minutes.

Timeline

1956	1959	1973	1981	1983
Born in Decatur, Alabama	*Moves to Chicago*	***Graduates** from high school*	*Earns medical doctor's degree from Cornell Medical School*	*Works in Africa with Peace Corps*

4

Years before, when Mae was a young girl, she announced that she wanted to be a scientist. She visited Chicago's Adler **Planetarium** and looked through the big telescope. She read **astronomy** books and adventure stories about space travel. She dreamed of traveling into space, and she worked hard to make her dream come true. When she grew up, Mae Jemison became the first African-American woman in space.

Mae saw a view like this of Earth from space.

1987	1992	1993	1994
Begins astronaut training	Flies on shuttle mission	Teaches at Dartmouth College; forms The Jemison Group, Inc.	Begins The Earth We Share science camp; establishes Dorothy Jemison Foundation for Excellence

Family

Mae Carol Jemison was born in Decatur, Alabama, on October 17, 1956. Her father, Charlie, was a carpenter and roofer. He often worked two jobs, but no matter how many hours he worked, he found time for his family. Mae's mother, Dorothy, stayed home to care for Mae, her sister Ada Sue, and her brother Ricky. When Mae was three, Dorothy moved the children to Chicago so she could finish college.

Mae, at age four, is shown here with her older sister Ada Sue and her brother Ricky.

Chicago, Illinois, is the third largest city in the United States.

Mae's father soon joined the family in Chicago. Most of Mae's early memories are of her life there. She considers Chicago her hometown. Mae is proud of her mother for going back to school and becoming an elementary school teacher. Mae's parents taught her that she could be whatever she wanted to be if she worked hard at her studies. She studied hard and got excellent grades.

Early Interests

Mae jumped and did flips all the time. Even though she loved to dance, Mae was clumsy. Her mother hoped dance lessons would help her to become more graceful. Mae was eight when she began ballet. She enjoyed the classes. A year later she took classes at the Jane Addams Hull House Center with a beautiful African-American woman named Mrs. Madison. The lessons made Mae feel strong and graceful.

Like these girls, Mae enjoyed dance class.

When Mae (back row, middle) was in high school, she joined the Modern Dance Club.

Mae knew how to read before she started school. Her mother read her stories, and books had always been part of her life. When Mae was in third grade, she began a science fair project showing how Earth changed over time. Mae spent hours in the library reading astronomy books and space adventures. She liked to look at the stars and imagine traveling in space. Mae did so well in school that she skipped seventh grade.

College

Mae **graduated** from high school about a year early at age sixteen. She decided to go to Stanford University in California. Mae studied to be a **chemical engineer.** She learned **Swahili,** a language of Africa, and earned a degree in African and African-American studies. She became the first woman president of Stanford's Black Student Union.

In college, Mae took a class on African dance. She created the dance routines for a college play. For a while, Mae thought about becoming a dancer.

Stanford University, shown here, is located in California, north of San Jose.

Nichelle Nichols starred as Lieutenant Uhura on *Star Trek.*

Mae continued to read and learn about space. Her favorite TV show was *Star Trek,* and she imagined herself traveling to the stars like **Lieutenant** Uhura. When Mae was about to **graduate** from college, a friend mentioned that **NASA** was looking for new astronauts.

Mae wasn't ready to join NASA. She decided to go to Cornell University Medical School in New York City. She hoped one day to use her knowledge of **chemical engineering** and medicine to find new ways to help people overcome illness.

Chemical Engineer

Chemical engineers help build and design chemical plants. They also use chemistry to improve food products, medicines, fuels, explosives, and other products made with chemicals.

Doctor

Mae enjoyed living in New York and studying medicine. During summer vacations she traveled to Cuba, Kenya, and Thailand to study how doctors in Africa and Asia help sick people and try to keep people well. Mae worked in hospitals and clinics taking care of sick people. In Kenya she walked from town to town checking the height and weight of children and finding out who needed vaccinations (medicines to protect them against diseases).

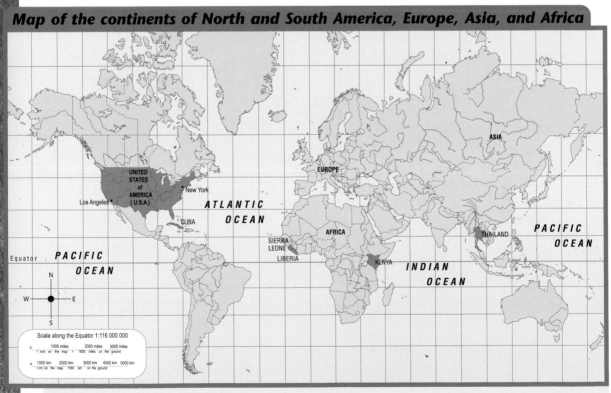

Map of the continents of North and South America, Europe, Asia, and Africa

UNITED STATES of AMERICA (U.S.A.)

New York

Los Angeles

CUBA

ATLANTIC OCEAN

EUROPE

ASIA

AFRICA

SIERRA LEONE

LIBERIA

KENYA

THAILAND

PACIFIC OCEAN

INDIAN OCEAN

Equator

PACIFIC OCEAN

N
W — E
S

Scale along the Equator 1:116 000 000

0   1000 miles   2000 miles   3000 miles
1 inch on the map = 1830 miles on the ground

0 1000 km 2000 km 3000 km 4000 km 5000 km
1 cm on the map 1160 km on the ground

This world map highlights important places in Jemison's life.

Dr. Jemison became a doctor so she could help people.

Mae **graduated** from medical school in 1981. She was now Dr. Jemison. She moved to Los Angeles where she worked in a hospital. In 1983, she returned to Africa as a Peace Corps doctor. She was sent to Sierra Leone and Liberia, where she worked to keep the Peace Corps volunteers and embassy staff healthy.

Dr. Jemison had never planned to practice medicine, but she discovered that she liked being a doctor.

Peace Corps

This government program, begun in 1961, sends American volunteers to help people in other countries.

15

The Decision

In 1985, Dr. Jemison returned to Los Angeles to practice medicine. She attended school in the evenings to study **biomedical engineering.** Even though she was busy working as a doctor and studying, she had not forgotten her dream to travel into space. In October she filled out an application to enter **NASA**'s astronaut training program. So did 2,000 other people.

This drawing shows a model of the space shuttle.

Astronaut Guion Bluford was the first African-American in space.

In the early days of space flight, all the astronauts had been military pilots. By the 1970s, NASA realized that they also needed scientists, called **mission specialists,** to travel into space. Mission specialists help with the day-to-day running of the space shuttle, and they also work on science experiments. Some of the mission specialists were women, and some were African-American men. But there were no African-American women astronauts. Dr. Jemison hoped to become the first.

Accepted!

On January 28, 1986, the space shuttle *Challenger* exploded just after it was launched from Florida. Seven astronauts died. **NASA** stopped its search for new astronauts until **experts** could find the reason for the explosion and fix the problem. Dr. Jemison felt sad about the shuttle explosion, but she still wanted to become an astronaut.

By February 1987, NASA was ready to consider new shuttle missions. They called Dr. Jemison and invited her to Houston for an **interview** and medical tests.

This picture shows the space shuttle *Challenger* ready for liftoff.

Jemison talked to reporters about becoming an astronaut.

In June 1987, Dr. Jemison learned that she had passed the tests. She was one of fifteen people chosen to begin astronaut training. NASA officials asked her not to tell anyone until the next day when it would be announced on the news. Jemison was too excited to keep the secret. She told her cat, Sneeze, that they would be moving to Houston to begin astronaut training. Sneeze didn't tell anyone else.

Training

The shuttle *Challenger* flies over the Johnson Space Center. The Johnson Space Center in Houston, Texas, is where astronauts train for space flight.

Dr. Jemison moved to Houston and began a year of training. She learned all about the space shuttle and the history of space flight. She took classes in **meteorology, geology,** and **astronomy.** She learned scuba diving, wilderness survival, and parachute jumping. Dr. Jemison hoped to become a **mission specialist** who would perform science experiments, so she learned all she could about day-to-day life on the shuttle.

The astronaut trainees learned about **weightlessness** by flying in a special jet, the KC-135. The airplane would fly high and then suddenly drop down. For 20 to 30 seconds, the astronauts would float through the air just like they would on a real shuttle mission. It gave them a chance to practice moving, eating, drinking, and working on the equipment without **gravity** holding them down.

Dr. Jemison became an astronaut in August 1988.

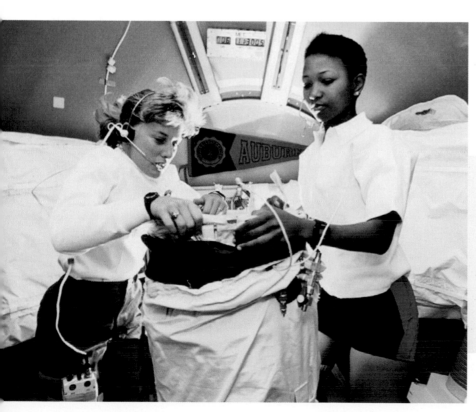

In this photo, Jemison and astronaut Jan Davis are training for flight.

Space Shuttle *Endeavor*

As a **mission specialist**, Dr. Jemison began work at the Johnson Space Center. She spent a year helping with other shuttle missions while she waited for one of her own. In 1989, she was assigned to the newest space shuttle, *Endeavor*. Her mission, *STS-47 Spacelab J*, was due to go into space in September 1992. Dr. Jemison spent her time training with the six other members of the crew.

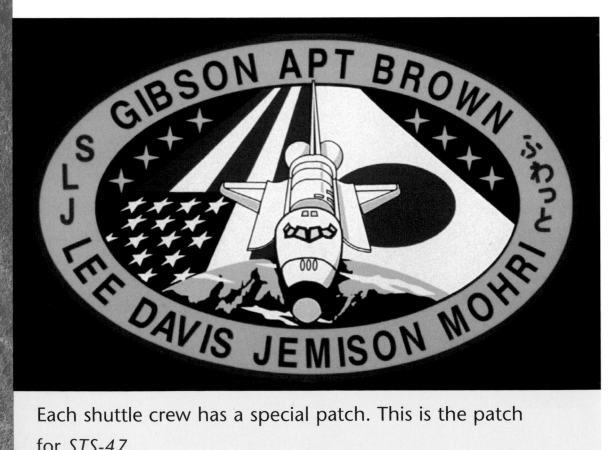

Each shuttle crew has a special patch. This is the patch for *STS-47*.

Jemison (second from left) is pictured here with her shuttle crew.

Dr. Jemison would be on the *Endeavor*'s second flight. Her mission was the 50th shuttle mission. Because the nation of Japan helped to pay for the shuttle, a Japanese astronaut, Dr. Mamoru Mohri, joined the crew. Dr. Jemison learned Japanese and took many trips to Japan to work on the experiments planned for the mission.

STS-47 Firsts

- *Mae Jemison was the first African-American woman in space.*
- *Mamoru Mohri was the first Japanese citizen in space.*
- *Mark Lee and Jan Davis were the first married couple in space.*

Space Flight

Dr. Jemison and the *STS-47* crew boarded the *Endeavor* on September 12, 1992. When it blasted into space, Mae Jemison smiled!

Dr. Jemison loved the feeling of **weightlessness** and didn't feel sick at all.

The space shuttle *Endeavor* lifts into space with Dr. Jemison aboard.

Space Sickness

About half of the astronauts who travel into space suffer from stuffy noses, headaches, and tiredness caused by weightlessness. Some lose their appetites or feel sick to their stomachs. This usually passes in a few days.

Dr. Jemison spent her days in space working on science experiments. One tested a new way of helping astronauts deal with space sickness. Another studied the way people's bones change in space. She did experiments with frog eggs to see if they could develop in zero **gravity**. The astronauts worked twelve-hour shifts. When she was not working or sleeping, Dr. Jemison looked out the shuttle windows at the Earth, the Moon, and the stars.

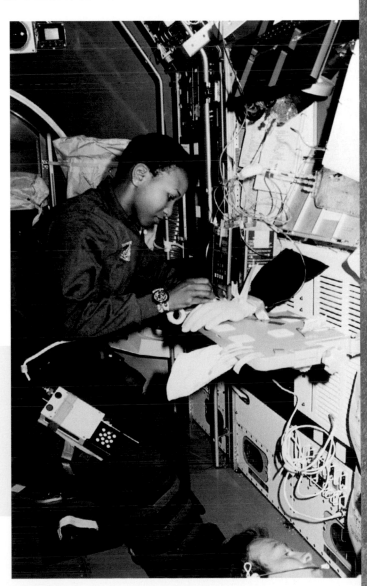

Dr. Jemison took part in many experiments while on the shuttle. Here she works on a medical experiment.

Welcome Home

STS-47 Spacelab J made 127 orbits of Earth and flew for 8 days. It landed on September 20, 1992.

Friends and family were waiting to welcome Dr. Jemison home. Newspaper, television, and radio reporters asked her questions. She shared her excitement about the space flight. On Dr. Jemison's 36th birthday, the city of Chicago held a six-day celebration in her honor. She spoke at her old high school and told the students to follow their dreams.

Minutes after launch, Dr. Jemison looked out the shuttle window to see a view like this of her hometown, Chicago.

Jemison attended the first showing of a *Star Trek* movie in Hollywood in 2002.

One of her own dreams came true when she appeared on the television show *Star Trek: The Next Generation* with her favorite character, **Lieutenant** Uhura. She also appeared on the *Oprah Winfrey Show* and was given the Ebony Black Achievement Award in 1992. In 1993, Jemison was listed as one of the "50 Most Beautiful People in the World" by *People* magazine and was **inducted** into the National Women's Hall of Fame in Seneca Falls, New York.

Ideas from Space

In 1993, Dr. Jemison left **NASA**. She started her own company, The Jemison Group, Inc. She hoped to use ideas from space to improve the lives of people in poor countries. The Jemison Group set up systems using energy from the Sun to provide cheaper heat and light for hospitals. They built systems that made it possible for doctors in small villages to get help from big city hospitals.

Dr. Jemison also taught Environmental Studies at Dartmouth College in Hanover, New Hampshire.

Dr. Jemison often speaks to groups about space travel and women in science.

This artist's drawing shows the space shuttle glowing as it returns to Earth.

In 1994, Dr. Jemison honored her mother by setting up the Dorothy Jemison Foundation. It was formed to help teachers make science fun and interesting in their classes. The foundation also runs an international science camp called The Earth We Share. Teens from all over the world meet together to talk about science and work on science projects. Dr. Jemison encourages students to follow their dreams wherever they may lead. Perhaps some of them will become space pioneers just like Mae Jemison.

29

Glossary

astronomy   study of the stars

biomedical engineering   use of science to improve health. Biomedical engineers work with things such as X rays, artificial arms and legs, and machines to measure breathing and heartrate

chemical engineer   scientist who uses chemistry for practical purposes

clinic   place people go for medical help

commander   person in charge

geology   study of rocks and minerals and the structure of the Earth

graduate   complete school

gravity   force that draws things toward Earth

interview   meeting when an employer or someone from radio, television, or the newspapers asks questions to find out about a person

lieutenant   military officer

meteorology   study of weather and climate

mission specialist   scientists who perform experiments on the space shuttle

NASA   National Aeronautics and Space Administration, the agency that studies and carries out work in space

planetarium   large dome that shows images of the Sun, Moon, stars, and planets on the inside of its walls

sickle cell anemia   blood disease that mostly affects African people

More Books to Read

Alagna, Magdalena. *Mae Jemison: The First African American Woman in Space*. New York: Rosen, 2004.

Naden, Corinne J. and Rose Blue. *Mae Jemison Out of This World*. Brookfield, Conn.: Millbrook, 2003.

Streissguth, Thomas. *Mae Jemison*. Mankato, Minn.: Bridgestone, 2003.

Places to Visit

Adler Planetarium & Astronomy Museum
1300 S. Lake Shore Drive
Chicago, Illinois 60605-2403
Visitor Information: (312) 922-STAR

The National Women's Hall of Fame
76 Fall Street
Seneca Falls, New York 13148
Visitor Information: (315) 568-8060

Index